Environmental Diseases

Madelyn Klein Anderson

ENVIRONMENTAL
DISEASES

A GROLIER COMPANY

FRANKLIN WATTS
NEW YORK|LONDON|TORONTO|SYDNEY|1987
A FIRST BOOK

88384

Photographs courtesy of: Monkmeyer: p. 10
(Ray Solomon); Photo Researchers, Inc.: pp. 14
(John Spragens, Jr.), 23 (Jonathan Watts/Science
Photo Library), 31 (Stan Levy), 34 (Guy Gillette),
49 (Joseph G. Hakey), 50 (Dr. Brian Eyden/Science
Photo Library); The Bettmann Archive, Inc.: pp. 19,
28; NASA: p. 20; Centers for Disease Control: p. 41;
EPA: pp. 47 and 54 (S. Delaney), 58.

Library of Congress Cataloging-in-Publication Data

Anderson, Madelyn Klein.
Environmental diseases.

(A First book)
Bibliography: p.
Includes index.
Summary: Examines how environmental factors such
as hazardous chemicals and radiation may cause a
variety of diseases.
1. Environmentally induced diseases—Juvenile
literature. [1. Environmentally induced diseases.
2. Diseases] I. Title.
RB152.A518   1987   616.9′8   87-8117
ISBN 0-531-10382-X

Contents

Chapter One
**Every Disease Is
an Environmental Disease**
9

Chapter Two
**Your Environment Guards
You Against Attack**
17

Chapter Three
Pandora's Box
27

Chapter Four
**Chemicals and Radiation
in Our Environment**
33

Chapter Five
**More about
Hazardous Chemicals**
45

Chapter Six
A Last Word
61

Glossary
63

For Further Reading
67

Index
69

Environmental Diseases

Chapter One

EVERY DISEASE IS AN ENVIRONMENTAL DISEASE

Today's your big day—and you wake up sick. Your head hurts. Your body seems too heavy to move. You're hot, then you're cold. You ache all over. "This is unbelievable," you groan. "Why today? Why me?"

Why, indeed?

Your environment is letting you down.

When you think of environment, you probably think of lakes and trees and Mother Nature. Your environment is much more than that—in fact, it's three environments: your outer environment, your inner environment, and the greater-world environment.

Your outer environment includes the air you breathe, the food you eat, the water you drink, the places in which you live and go to school and play, the groups to which you belong, your family, and all the people with whom you come in contact. Your internal or inner environment is within your body, shaped by your particular cells and your *genes*. Genes transmit the characteristics we inherit and in turn pass on to our descendants. Your life experiences, your knowledge and intelligence, your emotions, your mem-

ories, all build on your genetic foundation to shape your internal environment.

Your genes dictate the kind of body you have and how it will respond to your external environment. Your genes give you the strengths and weaknesses of your body and make you susceptible to certain diseases. People may not recognize a disease as genetic. Few people know even the names of all their eight great-grand-parents much less the illnesses they had. Some people are embarrassed to admit what they see as a family weakness. So the genetic link is often hard to demonstrate. Not every genetic possibility becomes reality, either. Females who carry the hemophilia gene do not get hemophilia (a disease that causes hemorrhaging, or heavy bleeding, particularly into the joints of the body), although they pass the gene on to their sons who do. Someone may inherit a gene for diabetes but never come down with the disease, because other factors in the environment do not trigger it off.

YOUR ENVIRONMENT STARTS BEFORE YOU ARE BORN

The environment of a fetus (an infant developing in its mother's womb) can cause disease and deformity. Infants can be born already addicted to drugs or suffering from venereal (sexual) diseases such as AIDS (Acquired Immune Deficiency Syndrome), passed to them from the bloodstreams of the mothers who carried them. Chemicals in the mother from excessive smoking or alcohol and some medicines can also damage the fetus. So can the virus of German measles. *Radiation* and accident are also environmental hazards to the fetus. Some of these hazards may affect genetic structure as well, so that the problem may be passed to future generations.

Prospective parents are given the opportunity to test for possible genetic flaws that will cause serious diseases or development disabilities in a child they might conceive. *Amniocentesis*, a test of fluid in the sac within which the fetus develops until it's ready to be born, is performed fairly routinely to uncover suspected genetic disease. Sometimes treatment is possible, or parents can choose to end the pregnancy.

The process of birth can cause disabilities in a newborn because of a flawed environment within the birth canal or poor delivery procedures. The newborn may get respiratory disease from anesthetics or drugs that sometimes must be given to the mother during delivery.

The environment of an unwanted newborn can also be contaminated by neglect. The baby who is not cuddled, who is ignored, can be seriously retarded mentally and physically, and, in extreme cases of deprivation, even die.

YOUR ENVIRONMENT IS UNIQUE

Your internal and external environments are like the two sides of a single page of this book; they cannot be separated. Your page is unique, like no one else's, now or ever. Your genes and experiences write a different story on your page, even if you are one of a pair of identical twins. You do share an environment with others, a greater-world environment that is like the cover of this book, sheltering all the pages. The world environment has disease and disasters that affect us in less obvious but still important ways. Radioactive fallout from the explosion and fire in an atomic reactor at Chernobyl in the Soviet Union may never have reached our immediate environment to make us sick. But we are still concerned for the atmosphere of our planet.

When we talk of disease and environment, all three of your environments are involved. Changes in one can cause changes in another, and each changes over the years. You age, you get hurt, you develop different relationships, live in different places, do different things. And sometimes your inner and outer environments may not get along too well. Can you imagine what would happen if this side of the page you are reading started fighting with the reverse side? Disaster! Well, the same thing happens to you. You get sick!

GETTING SICK ISN'T EASY

Most of the time your inner environment works smoothly to keep you protected and safe from the many *pathogens*—disease-causing bacteria, viruses, and fungi—in your outer environment. You can even have pathogens prancing around in your body and never feel sick. Your body can rid itself of a few cancer cells with no fuss at all—you would never even know about it. At least a dozen potential pathogens live quietly inside us and work to keep us from getting sick. The staphylococcus microorganism lives on our skin normally and helps prevent other bacteria from getting inside us, but a staph infection can be very dangerous indeed.

Getting sick involves some very complicated interaction between your internal and external environments. If too many pathogens invade your body or put out too much *toxin* (poison) for your inner environment to handle, of if you are susceptible to the pathogens because of your genes, or if one of your body systems is not functioning as well as it should, or if your outer environment is not providing you with the nourishment you need or does not allow you to rest or rains on you or chills you or does some other nasty thing, you will get sick. *Stress* is another trigger to sickness. It sort of opens the door for sickness to happen. Stress is an internal response to pressures from your external environment—a bad test coming up, family problems, friend problems, all kinds of worries. Maybe your big day was not something you were really looking forward to, and you were tense and anxious about it. Maybe you were depressed or dissatisfied with yourself. Maybe you had a fight, or your parents came down too hard on you for something.

The kind of sickness you get, how sick you get, and how long the sickness lasts depends on the strength of the pathogens and strengths of your environment, internal and external. And the sickness may leave you with changes in your internal environment that may be permanent—something in your body may work less efficiently or not at all. Or sometimes your internal environment may work better—you may be made immune to any further attack from these pathogens.

Sickness, disease, is also a matter of how you view it. Different people see diseases differently. Some people's inner environments send off alarm signals demanding immediate attention at the first sign of discomfort—dis-ease. On the other hand, there's the person who can function no matter what and can brag, "I've never been sick a day in my life," although we know he or she should have been home in bed any number of times. People in some primitive cultures have the symptoms of what seem to us terrible diseases, diseases that would send us into the hospital. But these people function very well within their environment and do not consider themselves sick—so, in a sense, they aren't.

Some scientists, therefore, feel that good health means something other than simply the absence of disease. They feel that good health means the ability of a person to function within his or her environment.

*A common sight in Japan is that
of people wearing protective
masks to ward off harmful germs.*

Chapter Two

YOUR ENVIRONMENT GUARDS YOU AGAINST ATTACK

To function well, to maintain comfort, our inner and outer environments must be at peace with one another, must meet each other's needs. Our internal environment does an amazing job of adjusting automatically to our needs. Sometimes, however, it works too hard or is pushed too hard. It isn't easy to keep up, because both internal and external environments change so frequently.

FIGHT-OR-FLIGHT

Have you ever woken up in fright from a nightmare? Most people have. Your heart pounded, you shook all over, you were perspiring but your mouth was dry. Then you realized there was nothing to be frightened of, and you relaxed in exhaustion. This reaction to danger, real or imaginary, is called "fight-or-flight." *Adrenaline* pours through your body, preparing you for quick and vigorous action, be it to stand and do battle or run away. Fat cells release fatty acids for instant energy. The acids also change to *lipopro-*

teins, needed to heal wounds. Your inner environment is protecting you against danger in your outer environment.

Fight-or-flight is a protective mechanism that we have inherited in our genes from the first human beings. They lived in hunting societies and had to face the constant danger of wild animals that they had to kill to eat or keep from being eaten. Most of us don't have to worry about things like that anymore, but we still carry the fight-or-flight mechanism in our genes. Fight-or-flight reactions are activated a lot in today's stressful world—when a car misses you by inches, being called on in class when you're not prepared, hearing a phone ring that you know means bad news. . . .

While fight-or-flight is a handy reaction to real danger, it's bad for the internal environment to be so continually overworked—and underused. Those unused lipoproteins hang around on the walls of the blood vessels with the unused fatty acids sticking to them, and eventually the circulatory system gets all clogged up.

A genetic trait that works well in the jungle can be a problem elsewhere. One day in the far future, humankind may have less sensitive fight-or-flight response systems. Genes that prevent adjustment to the environment tend to fade away, because the living things that carry them are weaker and survive in fewer and fewer numbers. Charles Darwin called this "survival of the fittest."

RESISTANCE AND IMMUNITY

Our genes lay down the pattern for the strength of our resistance to disease. But our environment over the years can increase or decrease that resistance. Having measles once will make us immune to measles forever. But having bronchitis usually means a weakening of our resistance to further attacks, and we will almost surely suffer from bronchitis again. Or medical science may immunize us against certain diseases, making our inner environment work at building up a resistance or barrier to more serious invasion. Unfortunately, not all diseases can be prevented by strengthening

Fight-or-flight. Our early ancestors' adrenaline must have been surging through their bodies most of the time as they struggled to survive in a hostile environment.

Quarantined Apollo II astronauts on their return from
the moon are greeted by President Richard Nixon,
who talks with them by microphone.
Scientists wanted to be sure the astronauts had not
brought back any harmful germs from space.

our inner environments. We can get an anti-flu injection, but flu viruses have a way of mutating, changing their genetic structure, so that our immune systems don't recognize them, and we just get sick with a different form of the same old disease.

While we are immune to certain pathogens because of previous exposure to them and can carry them around in our bodies without further harm, those pathogens can harm others who have never had any contact with them and so have never built any immunity to them. This is why babies are given immunization shots when they are so tiny. It is also why history tells of terrible epidemics brought by healthy European explorers to Eskimos, American Indians, Hawaiians, and other populations who died by the thousands of the new diseases like measles and whooping cough. This lack of immunity because of isolation is still a problem in remote areas. Scientists worried about astronauts bringing diseases to the moon, or bringing back strange pathogens that would devastate our world.

Perhaps it is no wonder that many scientists feel that city living is healthy living: there are so many pathogens going around that it is possible to build immunities to many diseases.

STABILITY OF THE INNER ENVIRONMENT

Infants are born with a special immune system that helps protect them from disease during the first six months or so of life. As tiny as infants are, their internal environments put up a great fight against pathogens, their temperatures zooming up to signal the battle in progress and quickly returning to normal in victory. Temperatures do not climb so fast or for so little reason as infants grow into babies, babies into children, children into adults. Other regulatory systems also stabilize, do not move up and down so wildly. This stability of the inner environment, called *homeostasis*, is essential to prevent disease and permit function. If our temperatures and the pressure of blood flowing in our arteries were always zipping up and down, if our bodies froze whenever the weather outside was freezing, or heated up to match the sizzling heat of the desert, we could not function. As a matter of fact, the human species would never have evolved at all were it not for homeostasis.

Suppose you walked out of a warm room into a snowstorm without putting on a coat. Your inner environment would change to protect you from your outer environment by trying to keep in your 98.6°F (37°C) of body heat. The blood vessels at the surface of your skin would constrict, narrow, so that the warm blood deeper inside would move to the cold surface more slowly, avoiding quick cooling. Your adrenal glands would secrete epinephrine to warm you and make you shiver. The shivering action of the tiny skin muscles would also serve to warm you. And when you ran back into the warmth of the house, your blood vessels would dilate, open wider, so that the inner warm blood could reach the cooler surface faster. You would perspire to further cool your skin. Finally, you would be fairly comfortable, all systems functioning normally in a state of homeostasis.

But if you were in an environment that pushed homeostasis beyond its capacities, that demanded too many adjustments too quickly, that overwhelmed it with too many pathogens or toxins, or gave it the wrong information as in the fight-or-flight reaction, homeostasis could break down. This is pathology, or disease. Homeostasis tends to break down a little more easily once you reach age thirty or so. By the time you're about seventy, it will be much more easily pushed beyond its capacities. With less stability of the internal environment, there is less resistance to disease. Enzymes that fight cancer cells, blood cells that fight infection, tissue repair and regrowth, gland functioning—all those things the body uses to protect itself against disease—don't work quite so well, don't respond so quickly, and are more overwhelmed by fewer attackers.

Some people are highly susceptible to allergens
in the environment. The results are often coldlike
symptoms: sneezing, a runny nose, and watery eyes.

TRICKSTERS

The inner environment can be fooled into fighting as if attacked by pathogens or toxins. *Allergens* are the substances that do the fooling, but the disease responses they cause, the allergies, are no laughing matter. Allergens cause hay fever, headaches, skin rashes, and a multitude of other problems. Some, like asthma and shock reactions, can be fatal. Allergens can be almost anything: pollen, dust, molds, smoke, medicines, sunshine, fabrics, animals, perfumes, sprays—the list can go on and on. Sometimes the body becomes so sensitized that the smoke coming from poison ivy that is burning hundreds of yards away can cause a breakout of poison ivy rash. Even the imagination can cause an allergy attack. In one well-known case a young girl allergic to daisies saw her father buying a bouquet of daisies in a department store and started to have a severe reaction until she was shown that the daisies were artificial.

Even without allergens, the mind can cause our internal environment to react as though attacked. Our minds, our emotions, can cause physical diseases as well as mental ones. Not too long ago people believed that people could die or be driven insane by grief or lost love—and people did seem to die because of unrequited love or go mad with grief. We don't do that anymore—we see and know the world differently, so we don't respond in those ways. But we still get disease responses that have no physical trigger. And we sometimes get well when we are given *placebos*, substances the doctor tells us are medicine, although they have no medicinal value and may be ordinary sugar. Placebos have been shown to produce real and measurable changes in several systems of the body.

How we view and respond to our external environment is a strong factor in physical as well as mental disease. Do we see it as threatening or as a challenge, as good or as bad? Are we very competitive or not competitive at all or somewhere in between? Do we get upset easily? Do we hide our upsets? How do we deal with demands, with problems, with losses? Do we need crutches like drugs or alcohol or are we able to handle life? The responses we make, the way we look at life and sickness, are part of every disease process. And while we may no longer die for love, we still get sick for emotional reasons.

Chapter Three

PANDORA'S BOX

Many children in the late 1930s went to school with a little bag of camphor and garlic around their necks to ward off polio. Presumably, the polio germs were meant to die from the smell. They didn't. And while none of the children died from the smell either, lots of children—and adults—died or were crippled by polio. Few people knew about viruses in those days. They blamed polio on "something" in the air.

From the time of the ancient Greeks, putrid or rotten air was blamed for disease. Letting in the night air was supposed to cause fever. After all, Pandora's curiosity had made her open that box when she shouldn't have, and all the diseases in the world had made their escape into the air.

TROUBLED AIR

While our ancestors were wrong about the air causing disease, they weren't far off the mark about it bringing disease. The mosquitoes, ticks, flies, and fleas that carry the germs that cause dis-

eases do fly—or hop—through the air. Someone sneezes and the spray travels through the air bringing lots of microscopic cold germs with it. Poisonous gases, both natural and artificial, and radiation travel through the air. But the air is simply a vehicle, and the pathogens and poisons are its passengers.

TROUBLED WATERS

Until the last century, most people did not understand that things they could not see in their water supply could make them sick. Many people still do not understand the relationship of water and disease, that you can get dangerously ill from typhoid and typhus and other diseases when you drink, bathe, defecate and urinate, and prepare food in the same body of water. Many people still don't know anything about proper preparation and storage of foods to avoid parasites, germs, and bacterial toxins or poisons.

TROUBLED WORLD

WHO (the World Health Organization of the United Nations), the U.S. Peace Corps, and other groups are teaching people in underdeveloped nations better sanitation as a safeguard against disease.

Developed countries, too, have their pockets of backward areas that are also targets for programs to improve health by improving the basics of care for environments, external and internal.

Agencies worldwide are also trying to fight starvation in these areas where the environment fails, where drought or flood or war—

The mythical Pandora opens the box containing humanity's many troubles and diseases.

the ultimate environmental disease—makes farming or hunting impossible, and poverty prevents the purchase of foods. Teaching crop cultivation and the use of alternative foods, like soy substitutes for meat, are long-term efforts to wipe out starvation. Distribution of free foods is an immediate remedy. Unfortunately, delivery of the foods is a tremendous problem—roads and landing strips for planes have to be built, railroads have to run, for food to reach the starving in undeveloped environments.

BEYOND THE BASICS

For the rest of us, the basics are taken care of—the water we drink is purified, and we understand the need to refrigerate and cook foods carefully. We understand how to guard against most infectious and contagious diseases, and we understand the importance of good health practices. But we are only just becoming aware that there are more dangers in our environment, more complex problems of disease and disease prevention, than we had ever realized.

We are learning of foods that may be harming us, not with toxins but with fats or chemicals that our bodies do not use properly. We are finding that chemicals in our air and water and land and homes not only pollute, but some cause disease—and some of those diseases are life-threatening. We are also hearing a lot about radiation effects and are even being advised to reject our physicians' recommendations for diagnostic X rays or other procedures

We used to give little thought to how many X rays we had, but today it is believed that too many can be harmful.

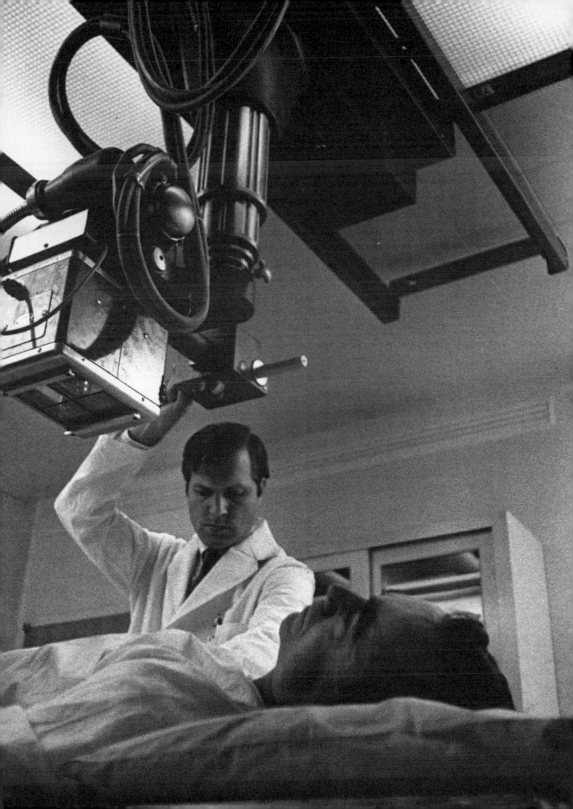

based on radiation. We are confused by the conflicts, by fear. We tend to believe whatever suits us best. We follow whoever makes the most skillful use of the media—newspapers, TV, radio—to convince us that there is nothing to fear or everything to fear. But what do we do when the government says it is all right to eat fruits that are exposed to gamma ray irradiation to eliminate bacteria and insects, and environmental groups say it is not? And do we get that X ray or not?

No one wants to sit around and wait while something might be done to eliminate sources of *carcinogens*, cancer-causing agents, or other threats to life and well-being. But which chemicals, what amount of radiation are threats and in what amounts? And what do we do about them? These chemicals and rays are as mysterious and frightening to us as the invisible bacteria and viruses must have been to earlier generations. Happily, scientists are at work in their laboratories just as they were back then, and one day they will solve the mysteries, just as they have before.

Chapter Four

CHEMICALS AND RADIATION IN OUR ENVIRONMENT

Chemicals can be natural or synthetic. Synthetic chemicals number in the hundreds of thousands, and thousands of new ones are produced every year. Some chemicals can cure disease, and some chemicals can cause disease or make a disease worse. Some chemicals can alter the genes that guide the reproduction of cells. Some chemicals can join with DNA in a cell to make it different from normal—a precancerous condition known as the "initiation stage." Other chemicals can bring about the next stage of cancer, called the "promotion stage," which can occur many years after the first exposure.

Cancer seems to be our primary worry when we consider chemicals in the environment, particularly since there are so many possible carcinogens and so many conflicting reports about them. The surgeon general of the United States says that no chemical substance should be considered safe without controlled animal studies. The surgeon general's office warns that any chemical that causes cancer in laboratory animals is potentially hazardous to human beings even if the danger to humans has not been proven.

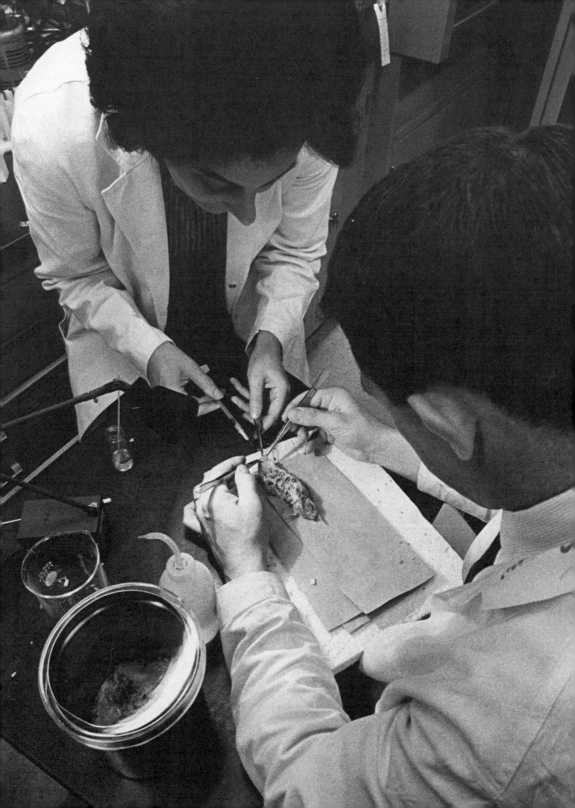

In case one experiment proves cancer and another does not, it is recommended that we accept the one positive for cancer. The surgeon general also states that any chemical proven to cause *benign*— noncancerous—tumors in animals should be considered a possible cause of cancerous growths in human beings. In other words, the surgeon general is saying it's better to be safe than sorry.

CHEMICALS IN WATER

Many of the thousands of chemicals in the environment enter our water supplies, usually in very small, harmless amounts. Most of the water we drink comes from surface sources—rivers, lakes, and streams—and is purified so that we can drink it safely. The chemical *fluoride* is also added to many water supplies to fight tooth decay, although a few people still object and blame fluoridation for all kinds of diseases, including AIDS. Animals also drink surface water, and fields are irrigated with water usually. Whether the chemicals that reach humans from these food crops and meats are dangerous to health seems to be a matter of opinion rather than proven fact.

Water also comes from wells that tap *groundwater*. Groundwater is the water beneath the ground that seeps in from rains and snows, feeding underground rivers and held in porous rocks. Chemicals enter both groundwater and surface water from illegal dumping of industrial wastes and accidental spills. Chemicals

Rodents are the primary laboratory animals used in cancer research. Here a research scientist and a lab technician examine a specimen.

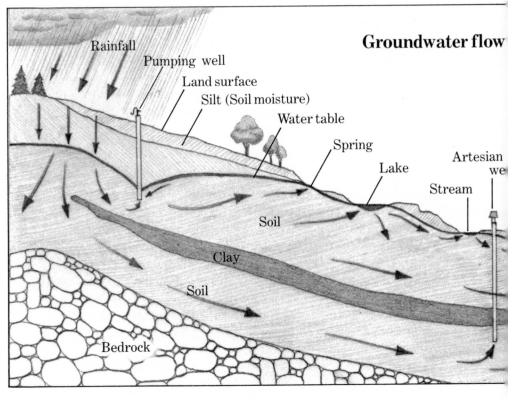

Groundwater flow

Rainfall
Pumping well
Land surface
Silt (Soil moisture)
Water table
Spring
Lake
Artesian we
Stream
Soil
Clay
Soil
Bedrock

*Follow the arrows from upper left to understand
this diagram of a typical groundwater system: Rainfall
penetrates the soil. Some fine soil is washed
downhill as silt. The rest seeps down as far as bedrock,
the solid support under the earth. Thus water
flows through porous soil, into springs, lakes, and
streams, and can be actively pumped out by a well.
If there is a layer of clay underground, the water
cannot penetrate it. Clay is too dense. To reach
this water, an artesian well must be dug, drawing
water up by pressure. And this is how chemicals
in rainfall reach drinking water.*

that evaporate into the air, or reach the air in the smoke of incinerated wastes or of industrial processes, return to the water—they pour down with rain and snow and enter surface water directly or through sewer systems, or enter groundwater after seeping into the earth. Sewer systems add many more chemicals to surface water: sewage is processed chemically, and petroleum chemicals are flushed into sewers from streets, driveways, and gas stations.

The United States in 1974 passed a Safe Drinking Water Act that provides for the Environmental Protection Agency (EPA) to monitor water supplies periodically for chemical pollutants from these sources.

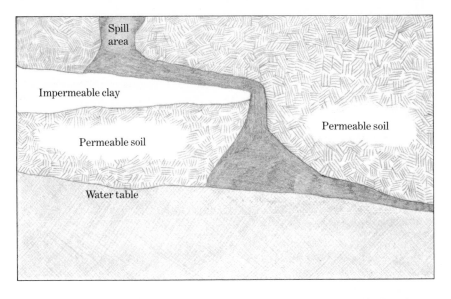

Chemicals spill onto the ground and seep into soil that is permeable—porous. If dense clay prevents seeping, the chemicals move laterally—sideways—until permeable soil is reached, and move down into the water table.

CHEMICALS IN THE AIR

The Clean Air Act of the United States recognizes (as of 1986) seven hazardous chemicals in the air: mercury, radon, beryllium, benzene, lead, arsenic, and polyvinyl chloride. These chemicals also enter water in the rain from the atmosphere. What happens when they enter the body in normal drinking water is not well documented, but they seem to be eliminated rather than stored up. But chemicals in the air enter the respiratory tract of the body, where, over the years, they can accumulate in the lungs, lowering immune response and possibly starting cancer or causing heart attacks and heart pain.

The United States monitors the air for sulfur dioxide (from sulfur-bearing fuels), nitrogen dioxide (from all fossil fuels), carbon monoxide (from engine combustion or fuel-burning), ozone, and particulate matter—chemical dust. (See Carbon Monoxide; Dust and Particulate Matter in chapter five.) A *Pollution Standard Index*, or *PSI*, rates the amount of pollution. A rating of under 50 indicates little pollution; 50–99, moderate pollution; 100–199, unhealthy; 200–299, very unhealthy; 300–399, hazardous; 400–500, very hazardous.

At the unhealthy level, most people find their eyes irritated, and they may have headaches. Those with heart or lung disease need to reduce activity. At the very unhealthy level more people will suffer distress, and the diseased and elderly should stay indoors. The hazardous and very hazardous ranges usually occur during warm, windless periods when the air acts like a cover holding in pollutants rather than dispersing them. At these times, everyone is advised to avoid the outdoors and decrease exercise. Diseases such as bronchitis, asthma, and heart problems may break out. The highest level of pollution can cause death in the chronically ill and elderly and symptoms of disease in even the healthiest of people. Everyone is advised to stay indoors with windows and doors shut, avoiding traffic and exertion.

*Smoke from an isolated dump carries
chemicals into the atmosphere.*

CHEMICALS IN THE EARTH

Burying wastes or fertilizing or spraying crops adds chemicals to the ground. We have seen how those chemicals can seep into groundwater and reach surface water, and some may enter the land food chain. Dumps that are used to bury hazardous wastes are of particular concern, especially when they are illegal and therefore uninspected, and their wastes are probably not properly contained. Many of these dumps were used years ago, before the toxicity of the wastes was known, and they are particularly frightening when discovered today. Indirect contact comes from seepage into water where they are diluted. Direct contact comes when kids play around dumps (an idiotic thing to do, and an unforeseeable hazard), or from building on top of them, a criminal offense. How much harm they cause is really not known, although they are highly suspect.

Many men and women who served in Vietnam claim that the numerous diseases they have, from acne to cancer, were caused by the chemical *Agent Orange*, recognized today as a carcinogen. Agent Orange was sprayed to destroy jungle growth concealing enemy troop movements. Whether all the diseases said to be caused by Agent Orange were actually caused by Agent Orange or by unknown pathogens or other chemical exposures over the years is still a matter of controversy—and publicity. Those veterans who banded together and brought a class-action legal suit against the federal government were awarded tiny damages. In effect, the courts were saying that Agent Orange might have caused all their problems but might not have. Compensation to true victims of Agent Orange is important and necessary. Compensation costs taxpayers great amounts of money. False claims, brought innocently by people who truly believe themselves victims or brought deliberately to get money, have to be weeded out to lessen the burden on the taxpayers—and to learn the truth about the dangers of chemicals in the environment.

Hazardous chemicals dumped at landfill
sites can poison our water supply.

Cleanup of toxic waste sites is costing the federal government—the taxpayers—something like $2 billion a year. Industry is finding ways to recycle or reduce their wastes, so there isn't so much to get rid of. Not only is it more efficient, it is more profitable and saves dumping costs, which are at present over $250 a ton (over $1,000 a ton when waste is incinerated and then buried). As populations grow and industries grow to serve them, we face the problem of more wastes and less place to put them. Recycling seems a good solution.

RADIATION

Like chemicals, radiation in our environment is both natural and manufactured, a blessing and a problem. We of course know of the horrors of radiation sickness as the result of atomic bombing or nuclear accident. But there are many other kinds of radiation. Without radiation there would be no world, no universe. The sun is a source of radiation, and so are the stars, and Earth itself.

Radiation is the emission (sending out) and movement of energy. Energy moves through space or some other medium in a wavy motion, rather like zigzagging on your bike or skates. You might make leisurely, long zigzags or tight, sharp patterns—and so does radiation. The pattern or length of the waves can be loose or tight, long or short, and is different in every form of energy. Sound is a form of energy that radiates in pressure waves. Electromagnetism is another form of energy. It radiates visible light; ultraviolet and infrared light; X rays; alpha, beta, and gamma rays; microwaves and radio waves.

When a wave of energy strikes an object, it causes that object to vibrate in the same wave pattern. Sometimes those vibrations are too strong for the object and break or change it. If the waves of sound that reach our ears are very strong and loud, as in a close bomb blast, our hearing mechanism will be injured and we can be deafened. In the same way, should strong electromagnetic radiation strike the molecules of DNA that make up our body, the DNA could be changed. Depending on factors we do not yet fully understand, this change can cause cancerous growths or sterility (inability to have children). Although sometimes blamed for causing birth defects, radiation rarely does, because the developing fetus damaged by radiation is usually aborted, lost, before birth.

Radio-frequency and microwave radiation are nonionizing radiations that occur naturally and also come from radar and radio-communication systems, TV transmitters, and microwave ovens. They may cause symptoms resembling stress, and in direct and close contact, as with a defective microwave oven, can cause severe burns.

Earth has electromagnetic fields that birds may depend on in long migratory flights. There is electromagnetic activity in muscle tissue, measured by electromyography, or EMG; in brain cells, measured by electroencephalograph, or EEG; and in heart muscle, measured by electrocardiogram, or EKG—all important diagnostic tools for disease and injury. There is no apparent effect on human beings of electromagnetic energy in the greater environment—in electrically driven subways, buses, and railways, and electric and telephone wires. But a number of European countries have set up precautionary guidelines for its use.

Ionizing radiation is atomic or nuclear radiation. It, too, occurs naturally—in the decay of uranium and other radioactive elements in the earth—and it is produced by X-ray tubes. Ionizing radiation is found in a number of products we use every day: TV sets, the luminous dials of watches and clocks, radioactive smoke detectors, glassware, earthenware, cement, and other building products made from earth. But those same building materials shield us from radiation from earth and sun. In treating disease, ionizing radiation is used for X-ray diagnosis, radiation therapy, and radioactive medicines. Ionizing radiation is present in nuclear weapons and nuclear fuel, but it is also present, in lesser amounts, in coal burned for fuel. Coal contains uranium, and when uranium is burned it produces ionizing radiation.

Chapter Five

MORE ABOUT HAZARDOUS CHEMICALS

The chemicals listed below are health hazards in large amounts. The general population is not normally exposed to large amounts, although buildup and accidental spills of larger amounts are possible. An exception is *particulate matter*, whose presence is readily visible and almost always protected against.

Many hazardous chemicals are not listed here. While individuals working with them can be harmed in accidents, the general population ordinarily has no exposure to them. There are, however, extraordinary accidents such as the one at a chemical processing plant in Bhopal, India, in 1985, that killed or disabled some two thousand people living near the plant. There are also natural disasters that spew chemicals from nature's depths: earthquakes, volcanoes, or the sudden upsurging of poisonous gas from the depths of a lake, as happened in Cameroon, Africa, in 1986.

Here, in alphabetical order, not order of importance, are the chemicals that most concern us:

ARSENIC

Arsenic is a highly poisonous metallic element when taken into the digestive tract, although people have been known to eat small amounts daily for years, their systems adjusting to it. Arsenic is found in weed killers, insecticides, and various alloys (combinations of metals). The Clean Air Act lists arsenic as hazardous.

ASBESTOS

Asbestos can be found in ceiling tiles, vinyl floor tiles, spray-on insulation, insulating boards, brake linings, fireproof fabrics, asphalt, with cement in flooring and shingles, as covering for pipes, in paper for electric insulation. Asbestos is a fire retardant, a feature that until a relatively short time ago was considered so important that most building codes demanded its use. But asbestos dust and fibers can accumulate in the lungs and are not removed by the normal processes of producing sputum and coughing. This leads to *asbestosis*, a form of *pneumoconiosis*, or pneumonialike disease, that can be fatal. There are conflicting opinions on asbestos as a carcinogen.

BERYLLIUM

A lightweight metallic element, beryllium is used in the manufacture of fluorescent lamps, in the aerospace industry and nuclear reactors, and mixed with copper for springs and nonsparking electrical contacts and tools. Listed by the Clean Air Act as a hazardous pollutant, its limited use makes it of less concern to the general public. However, to those working with it, protection is essential to avoid inhalation which can lead to acute and often fatal pneumoconiosis. (See also Dust and Particulate Matter.)

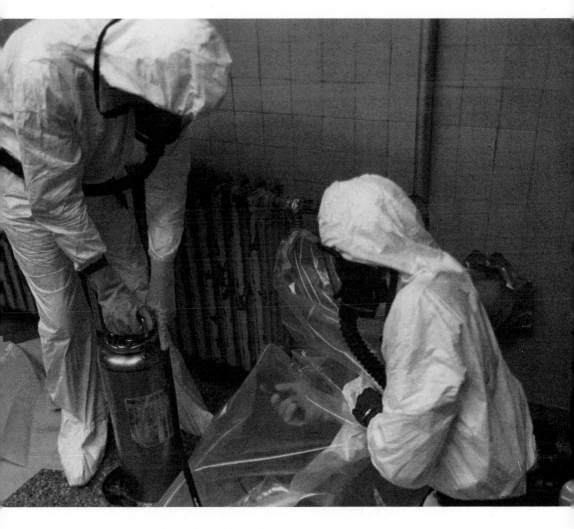

*Workers, wearing protective clothing and
oxygen masks, prepare to remove tiles
containing asbestos from a school building.*

CARBON MONOXIDE

This gas can attach to the red blood cells, preventing oxygen from reaching them. In sufficient amounts, it can, therefore, cause death. Running automobile engines in closed garages is a well-known cause of carbon monoxide buildup. Carbon monoxide also comes from the burning of charcoal indoors and faulty home heaters. Carbon monoxide is used in chemical processes, metal smelting, and as a fuel. Its presence in the air is monitored in the Pollution Standard Index.

DUST AND PARTICULATE MATTER

Keeping dust away is impossible even for the most energetic of housekeepers. Dust carries *particulate matter*—minute particles of soil, bacteria, molds, mites, propellant gases from aerosol cans, lead and carbon from vehicle exhausts, and soot and ash that enter buildings through air-conditioning systems and open windows, and other very tiny matter. The smaller the particulate matter, the more cause for concern, because it can dodge the body's defenses and lodge deeper in the lungs. Pneumoconiosis results.

Industrial particulate matter was a bad problem until recognized in the 1920s and is now generally protected against. Coal dust, for instance, settled into the lungs of many miners and caused *silicosis*, or *black lung disease*, a form of pneumoconiosis in which the air sacs of the lungs are gradually destroyed until not enough oxygen circulates to the body and the victim dies. Other industries, like quarrying, woodworking, bricklaying, demolition, also give off particulate matter that can cause pneumoconiosis. (See also Asbestos.)

Some chemical particulate matter can cause skin diseases. (See also Gaseous Oxides.)

People who work in the demolition industry risk the danger of contracting pneumoconiosis, a disease of the lungs.

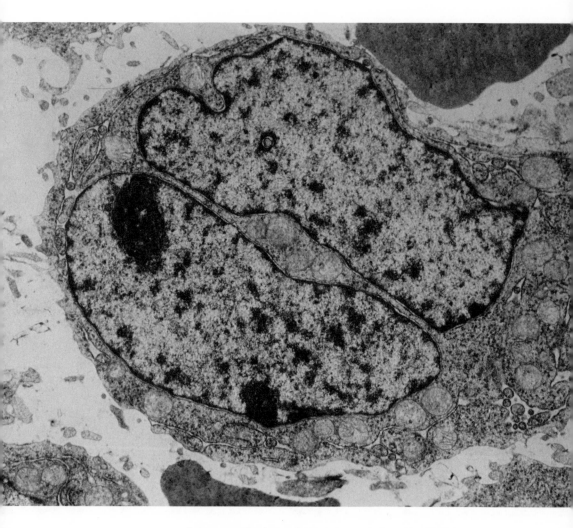

A transmission electron micrograph (TEM) of a deformed nucleus in a human cancer cell. A normal nucleus is round or oval; this one appears to have split in two.

FLUOROCARBONS

These are combinations of fluorine and carbon. Large numbers of these compounds are known. They are useful as solvents, insulators, and lubricants. Unfortunately they are also used as propellants for spray cans and can cause nausea and even unconsciousness when inhaled, and may be carcinogens.

FOOD CHEMICALS

The role of diet in causing or preventing certain diseases is receiving increasing attention. Caffeine in tea and coffee has been implicated in heart disease and bladder cancer. Saccharin is a possible carcinogen, and peanut butter often contains small quantities of aflatoxin, a serious allergen. Cured meats like bacon and sometimes ham and beef cuts, smoked fish, beer, and scotch whiskey contain sodium nitrite to prevent the growth of bacteria that cause botulism, a sometimes fatal food poisoning. Sodium nitrite is found naturally in our saliva, but if it combines with other chemicals in foods it becomes *nitrosamine*, a strong carcinogen. That is why there are objections to fruits and vegetables grown in fields fertilized with nitrates.

Cancers related to diet are estimated by some to be as high as 30 to 40 percent in men and 60 percent in women. High-fat diets seem related to breast, prostate, and large-intestine cancer. Animal fats and some oils can cause an increase of *cholesterol* in the body. Cholesterol is a chemical substance, white and soapy in appearance, that is in all of our tissues. Excess amounts can clog the arteries, making it more difficult for blood to circulate and causing increased blood pressure and heart disease.

High protein intake may be associated with cancer. Too high an intake of sugar and starches for the amount of insulin the pancreas can manufacture results in diabetes. Salt, which is mostly sodium chloride, tends to cause the tissues of the body to hold in fluids—bad for the kidneys, heart, and lungs. Salt elevates blood pressure, but is good for preventing heat stroke and dehydration, loss of too much body fluid.

Alcoholic beverages taken in excess not only can cause cirrhosis, or hardening, of the liver so that it stops functioning properly, which results in death, but also seem to be connected with colon and rectal cancer.

There is some question as to whether high-temperature cooking, such as broiling, and smoking or charcoal broiling produce carcinogens on the surface of the foods being cooked.

Not everything is bad—it only seems that way sometimes. High-fiber diets seem to reduce the risk of colon cancer. And, contrary to popular belief, some food preservatives can actually be good for you. BHA (butylated hydroxyanisole) and BHT (butylated hydroxytoluene), used to keep fats and oils from spoiling and to prevent changes in the color and flavor of foods, seem to help prevent the start of certain cancers and viral infections.

FORMALDEHYDE

Formaldehyde is a suspected carcinogen. Fabrics for clothing, curtains and drapes, upholstery, and carpets are treated with formaldehyde, sometimes in such large amounts that the smell is irritating. It is also an irritant when you don't smell it. (See Gaseous Oxides.) Formaldehyde is also used in plywood and particle board and some foam insulation. Its use in insulation was banned in 1982 by the federal government's Consumer Product Safety Commission.

GASEOUS OXIDES

Coal, petroleum (oil), and natural gas are fossil fuels. They come from deposits of fossils, the remains of small plants and animals that died in swampy, marshy areas many thousands of years ago.

Gasoline and benzene and many synthetic products are made from petroleum. Burning untreated fossil fuels gives off gaseous oxides—oxygen mixed with carbon, nitrogen, and sulfur. These oxides are carbon monoxide (see Carbon Monoxide), carbon dioxide, nitrogen dioxide, and sulfur dioxide. When nitrogen dioxide and sulfur dioxide mix with water in the air, they turn to nitric acid and sulfuric acid, acids that burn. Mixed with sunlight, the dioxides turn into irritants—formaldehyde, acrolein, ozone—that hurt the nasal membranes (the moist tissues that line the nose), the eyes, throat, and lungs.

Many governmental controls regulate the burning of fossil fuels and engine emissions, and the quality of air in cities like London (once notorious for its killing pea-soup fogs), Los Angeles, and Pittsburgh has improved tremendously. But to clean up the air around them, industries built taller chimney stacks to vent the smoke into the higher atmosphere where air currents disperse it. So sulfuric and nitric acids, ozone, and acrolein travel long distances and fall in *acid rain* on the vegetation and waters of furious neighbors.

The greatly increased amount of carbon dioxide released into the atmosphere by the burning of fossil fuels also tends to trap the heat reflected by the earth. This is known as the "greenhouse effect" because heat is held in as effectively as in a glass-enclosed greenhouse where plants are nurtured. Scientists are concerned about the greenhouse effect changing climates by changing temperature, rain, and wind patterns, and possibly damaging the ozone layer of the higher atmosphere. Some scientists also worry about the long-term effect on the polar regions of a rise in temperature—the polar ice caps could melt and raise the levels of the oceans, causing flooding of all the land bordering the oceans.

During the energy crisis, when Arab countries raised the price of their oil so much that countries dependent on that oil were put into economic chaos, many people turned to alternative energy sources. They used wood stoves and solar energy systems for heat-

ing homes. People weatherproofed their homes to prevent loss of heat in cold weather so that less fuel would be needed. Some time afterward it was realized that woodsmoke contained toxic heavy metals and at least a dozen known carcinogens. The better the care taken in weatherproofing, the more pollutants were trapped inside the building where they could cause more problems than when they dispersed in the atmosphere. Air exchange systems can help, but they are expensive.

LEAD

A poisonous element, lead is one of the heavy metals. (Copper, zinc, molybdenum, mercury, and cadmium are others.) Lead is widely used in industry because it is easily shaped into different forms. Lead lines storage tanks and pipes, and it is also used to make paper. It is used in making auto batteries and some gasolines to prevent the knocking sound as the engine runs. Lead can be part of paints, glazes, solder, and glass. Lead in most paints is now prohibited, but old lead paint on walls is still a serious source of lead poisoning, particularly in children and animals, who tend to put everything into their mouths. In its mildest form, lead poisoning resembles flu. More severe cases have symptoms of pain in the joints and abdomen and anemia—a reduction in the number of red blood cells, which carry oxygen essential to the life of the body's tissues. In the worst cases of lead poisoning, the cells of the brain are affected, causing irritable, peculiar behavior and retardation.

Gaseous oxides vented by industrial smokestacks into the atmosphere can poison the environment many miles away.

MERCURY

A poisonous element and one of the heavy metals, mercury is used alone or in combination with other elements. Mercury is found in chemical pesticides, thermometers, barometers, mercury suntanning lamps, antiseptics, and germicides. It is also used in photography, the making of pigments or coloring agents for paints and dyes, and metalwork. Powdered forms of mercury are particularly dangerous, because they can be inhaled and lodge in the lungs. (See Dust and Particulate Matter.) Any compound with mercury in it can damage the kidneys. Mercury, also known as quicksilver, is the only metal that is a liquid at ordinary temperatures. If you ever break a mercury thermometer (many are made with alcohol instead), don't try to pick the mercury up with your bare hands. Mercury is very poisonous and can be absorbed through the skin.

Disposal of mercury is a major environmental concern. Dumping into waterways was banned in 1976 because the mercury entered into the systems of fish. Concern was not so much for the fish, who seemed to suffer no ill effects, perhaps because of the selenium in their systems, but for human beings who ate the fish. We, too, have selenium in our bodies, but whether it is protective against mercury in food is not known. Nor is it known whether mercury that is buried enters the land food chain, seeping into the ground and entering into food plants and into animals that are eaten by human beings.

PCBs
(POLYCHLORINATED
BIPHENYLS)

There are PCBs in the tissues of most living things. The manufacture and sale of PCBs have been forbidden in the United States since 1979 because they are suspected of being a carcinogen. They are still around in generators, transformers, and large electrical equipment in the United States and will be for long years to come. Other countries are still using PCBs in manufacturing lubricants, solvents, and adhesives. The Environmental Protection Agency estimates that 10 million pounds (4.5 million kg) of PCBs enter the world environment every year, through leaks and dumping. PCBs are very stable—they have a very long life—and build up over the years into formidable amounts. Some species of fish can store more PCBs than are found in the water around them, and PCBs reach human beings through the food chain in the water. PCBs also reach the human body through the land food chain when fish are dried and ground into fertilizer for crops. People have been accumulating PCBs since infancy, and mothers' milk has been found to have more PCBs than bottled milk.

POLYVINYL CHLORIDE (PVC), ALSO CALLED VINYL CHLORIDE

PVC is a carcinogen found in plastics, in new shower curtains, upholstery, records, garden hoses, wrappings, credit cards, car seats, and some pipes. The Clean Air Act of the United States lists PVC and six other air pollutants as hazardous: asbestos, mercury, beryllium, benzene, radon, and arsenic.

RADON

Radon is a gaseous element formed in the course of the normal decay of the element radium. Radon is used in radiotherapy treatment for disease. In large amounts it can cause radiation sickness of varying intensity from nausea and headache to hair loss, anemia, hemorrhaging, and death. It tends to bond with dust and so can lodge in the lungs.

Radon is found everywhere in the soil, sometimes in larger amounts in pockets measuring hundreds of miles. One such pocket

AREAS WITH POTENTIALLY HIGH RADON LEVELS

extends from central Pennsylvania into southern New York State. Radon is found in all building materials with an earthen basis, like brick, tile, cinder blocks, concrete, adobe, stone. Homes that use a lot of stone and concrete to store solar energy retain the most radon.

Do-it-yourself kits for testing radon levels are being marketed, and ventilating systems are available to disperse house radon gas into the outside air. We cannot avoid exposure to radon, because we cannot house the world in tents and log cabins—and they, too, would probably be found to have one carcinogen or another. We cannot vacate all the cities built on pockets of radon, nor is it necessary. Unfortunately, hysteria seems to be building about radon. Lawsuits are being brought to gain damages for what seems to be good building practices—making homes airtight and energy-efficient—and for what Mother Nature is responsible but can't pay for.

VOLATILE ORGANIC COMPOUNDS (VOCs)

VOCs are carbon compounds that evaporate readily. Carbon compounds exist in huge numbers and are part of all living and many

The shaded areas on the map represent those areas that may have a greater percentage of houses with high radon levels. But other factors must be considered as well, such as whether the soil is permeable or not and how the houses are constructed.

nonliving things. Therefore, scientists look for evidence of carbon compounds when searching for signs of life in space.

VOCs evaporate into the air and descend with rain and snow into the waterways, or are dumped and sometimes leak from defective containers. VOCs come from factory wastes, dry-cleaning agents, solvents, pesticides, fire extinguisher contents, the wastes of leather tanning processes, and pharmaceuticals. Containers for these wastes can cost many thousands of dollars, which can lead to illegal dumping by companies that feel they cannot afford the expense.

Chapter Six

A LAST WORD

Technological advances have brought us electricity and automobiles and planes. We could not manage today without electric light, but because we can turn night into "day" we disturb natural biological rhythms that were attuned for millions of years to far shorter periods of light. We are equally dependent on cars and trucks and buses, and their engine exhausts are causing problems in the atmosphere and descending in the rain and snow into our water supply. More and more of us have the money and the leisure time to travel in planes, and we jet through time zones, which tends to disorient us.

Advances in space technology have brought human beings into an altogether new environment. The first astronauts were isolated upon their return to Earth to make sure they didn't bring any alien diseases back with them. They didn't, but they did bring back problems of weightlessness and calcium loss and motion sickness. Aquanauts are exploring the environment of the oceans, possibly more dangerous than outer space, and are also discovering the problems of adjusting their internal to their external environments.

We will not give up the benefits of technology, of space and underwater travel and life. We cannot and should not turn back the pages of history to achieve some idealized version of "clean" air and water and absence of radiation—we'd have to go back to the cave and then there would be radon and carbon monoxide and radiation and a dozen other pollutants there anyway, and no medicines. . .

We human beings will, over time, adapt to those things in the external environment that we cannot change. And we will change our environment to serve us better. We cannot possibly rid the environment of all disease, but we can improve the quality of all three of our environments immeasurably—with time.

Glossary

Acid rain: Rain or snow carrying sulfuric and nitric acids, ozone, and acrolein into the waterways, both directly and by runoff from the ground. These chemical pollutants reach the atmosphere in smoke from the chimneys of industries using combustion processes and in the exhausts from internal combustion engines in motor vehicles.

Adrenaline (the better-known name for epinephrine): A hormone or secretion of the adrenal gland. Adrenaline is secreted when sudden emotion or physical action stimulates the autonomic nervous system that controls our internal organs. That system then stimulates further secretion of adrenaline, setting up a circular reaction. Adrenaline prepares the organs of the body to react to emotional and physical triggers in the environment. Continued environmental stresses in the modern world that cause over-secretion of adrenaline and other hormones in the adrenal gland can cause disability of the gland and thus disease.

Agent Orange: A chemical defoliant, sprayed or dusted on plant growth to make the foliage—leaves—fall off.

Allergens: Substances that cause physical reactions in persons sensitive to them through touch, inhalation, or ingestion. Allergic reactions may also be caused by mental and emotional factors that seem to release chemicals in the body that act as allergens.

Amniocentesis: Test of the fluid in the sac within which a fetus develops. The fluid can be studied to determine possible birth problems or malfunctions and genetic abnormalities.

Asbestosis: See Pneumoconioses.

Benign: Characterizes a tumor or growth that is noncancerous.

Black lung disease: See Silicosis.

Carcinogens: Cancer-causing chemical compounds.

Cholesterol: Chemical fatty substance that accumulates in the tissues of the body. Cholesterol buildup contributes to the thickening and hardening of arteries carrying blood from the heart. When the blood supply to a part of the body is blocked by this accumulated material, either by closing the walls of a blood vessel or by a piece breaking off and traveling to a smaller blood vessel and blocking it, the result may be a stroke or a heart attack or other dangerous condition, depending on location.

Fluoride: Chemical used in a compound with other chemicals and added in very tiny amounts to public water supplies to prevent dental caries (cavities).

Genes: The physical units of heredity.

Groundwater: Water below the surface of the earth at varying depths. The upper level of the water is called the *water table.*

Homeostasis: Stability of the inner environment, particularly in relation to the many variations in the external environment. Numerous self-regulating systems within the body contribute to homeostasis.

Lipoproteins: Proteins made with fatty acids and other substances known as lipids.

Nitrosamine: Sodium nitrite, a chemical, mixed with other chemicals called amines. Nitrosamines are carcinogens.

Particulate matter: Very tiny pieces or particles of substances in the atmosphere—smoke, soot, ash, dust, aerosol sprays, and the residue from grinding, quarrying, demolition, and milling operations.

Pathogens: Disease-causing bacteria, viruses, and fungi.

Placebos: Substances offered as medicines that have no medical value—"sugar pills" or colored and flavored water. Used in testing for true effects of drugs and sometimes for patients whose symptoms may be imaginary.

Pneumoconioses (Singular: *pneumoconiosis*): Pneumonialike diseases of the lungs caused by inhalation of dusts—particularly those containing silica, asbestos, coal, raw cotton, and sugar cane waste—and of beryllium. *See also* Silicosis.

Pollution Standard Index (PSI): A U.S. government rating of amounts of pollution in the air and levels of danger they represent to the population.

Radiation: The emission of rays. Ionizing radiation is the emission of rays from nuclear sources.

Silicosis: A pneumonialike disease caused by inhalation of silica dust from pottery, metal grinding, sandblasting, and mining in rock. When caused by the dust from coal (anthracite) mixed with small amounts of silica, the disease is sometimes called anthracosis, better known as black lung disease.

Stress, emotional: An internal response to pressures from the external environment. Stress can produce any number of disease symptoms ranging from mild to severe, varying with the individual's internal environment.

Toxin: Poisonous substance of vegetable, animal, or bacterial origin.

For Further Reading

Dubos, Rene & Pines, Maya & Editors of Time-Life Books. *Health & Disease* (Rev. Edition, 1971). Alexandria, Va., Silver Burdett Co., School & Library Distributors, 1986. (Adult, but easy reading)

Gutnik, Martin J. *Ecology*. New York: Franklin Watts, 1984.

Legator, Marvin, et al, eds. *The Health Detective's Handbook: A Guide to the Investigation of Environmental Health Hazards by Nonprofessionals*. Baltimore: Johns Hopkins University Press, 1985. (Adult)

Miller, Christine G., and Louise A. Berry. *Wastes*. New York: Franklin Watts, 1986.

Norwood. Chris. *At Highest Risk: Environmental Hazards to Young and Unborn Children*. New York: McGraw Hill, 1980. (Adult)

Pringle, Laurence. *Lives at Stake: the Science and Politics of Environmental Health*. New York: Macmillan, 1980.

Sabin, Francene. *Ecosystems and Food Chains*. Mahwah, N.J.: Troll Associates, 1985.

Schwartz, Bert. *Pesticides: Mist of Death* (new edition). West Haven, Conn.: Pendulum Press, 1971.

Turner, Stephen. *Our Noisy World*. New York, Julian Messner, 1982.

Index

Italicized page numbers indicate illustrations.

Acid rain, 53, 63
Adrenal glands, 22
Adrenaline, 17, 19, 63
Aflatoxin, 51
Agent Orange, 40, 64
AIDS 11, 35
Alcohol, and fetus, 11
Alcoholic beverages, 52
Allergens, 25, 64
Alpha rays, 42
Alternative energy sources, 53–55
Alternative foods, 30
Amniocentesis, 11–12, 64
Arsenic, 38, 46
Asbestos, 46, 64

Asthma, 24

Bacteria, and sickness, 13
Bacterial toxins, 29
Benign tumors, 35, 64
Benzene, 38
Beryllium, 38, 46
Beta rays, 42
BHA, 52
Bhopol, India, 45
BHT, 52
Black lung disease, 48, 64
Blood pressure, 22
Blood vessels, and homeostasis, 22
Botulism, 51
Bronchitis, 18

Caffeine, 51

Cameroon, Africa, 45
Cancer, and BHA and BHT, 52; and chemicals, 33; of the colon and rectum, 52; and diet, 51; and high protein intake, 51
Carbon, 51
Carbon compounds, 59–60
Carbon dioxide, 53
Carbon monoxide, 38, 48, 53
Carcinogens, 32, 64; Agent Orange as, 40; asbestos as, 46; fluorocarbons as, 51; and high temperature cooking, 52
Cells, and inner environment, 9–10
Chemicals, in the air, 38–39; in the earth, 40–42; in environment, 33–42; hazardous, *41*, 45–60; and soil seepage, *37*; in water, 35–37
Chernobyl, Soviet Union, 12
Cholesterol, 51, 64
Circulatory system, 18
Cirrhosis of the liver, 52
Clean Air Act of 1986, 38, 57; and arsenic, 46; and beryllium, 46
Consumer Product Safety Commission, 52

Darwin, Charles, 18
Diabetes, and diet, 51

DNA, changes in, 33; and radiation, 43

Electrocardiogram (EKG), 43
Electroencephalograph (EEG), 43
Electromagnetic fields, 43
Electromagnetism, 42
Electromyography (EMG), 43
Epidemics, 21
Epinephrine, 22
Environment, adaptation to, 62; beginning of, 11–12; changes in, 12–13; and chemicals, 33–42; dangers of, 30–32; defined, 9; failure of, 29–30; functioning within, 15; kinds of, 9; protection of, 17–26; and radiation, 43–44
Environmental Protection Agency (EPA), 37, 57
Enzymes, protection of, 22
External environment, adjustment to, 61; perception of, 24–25; relation of to internal environment, 17–26

Fat cells, 17–18
"Fight or flight," 17–18, *19*
Flu viruses, 21
Fluoride, 35, 64
Fluorine, 51
Fluorocarbons, 51
Food chain, 40

Food chemicals, 51–52
Formaldehyde, 52
Fossil fuels, 52–55
Fungi, and sickness, 13

Gamma rays, 42
Gaseous oxides, 52–*55*
Genes, 64; and inner environ-
  ment, 9–10; and pathogens,
  13; and protective mecha-
  nism, 18
Genetic foundation, 11
German measles, 11
Germs, 27–29
Greater-world environment, 9,
  12; and electromagnetic en-
  ergy, 43
Groundwater, *35*–37, 65

Hazardous waste dumps,
  40–42
Hemophilia, 11
High fiber diets, 52
Homeostasis, 21–22, 65

Immunity, 15, 18–21
Infrared light, 42
Inner (internal) environment,
  9–10; adjustment to, 61; re-
  lation of to external environ-
  ment, 17–26; stability of,
  21–23; and tricksters, 24–25
Insulin, 51
Ionizing radiation, 43
Isolation, and immunity, 21

Lead, 38, 55
Light, ultraviolet, 42
Lipoproteins, 17–18, 65

Measles, 18, 21
Mercury, 38, 56
Microwaves, 42, 43

Nitric acid, 53
Nitrogen dioxide, 38, 53
Nitrosamine, 51, 65
Nonionizing radiation, 43
Nuclear accident, 42

Outer (external) environment,
  19; and nourishment, 13
Ozone, 38

Pancreas, 51
Pandora's box, 27, *28*
Parasites, 29
Particulate matter, 38, 45, 48,
  65
Pathogens, 13–15, 65; in the
  air, 29; and homeostasis, 22;
  and immunity, 21; and sick-
  ness, 15
Pathology, defined, 22
PCBs, 56–57
Peace Corps, 29
Placebos, 24, 65
Pneumoconiosis, 46, *49*, 65;
  caused by beryllium, 46; and
  particulate matter, 48
Polio, 27

Pollutants, 30–32
Pollution ratings, 38
Pollution Standard Index (PSI), 38, 65; and carbon monoxide, 48
Polyvinyl chloride (PVC), 38, 57
Protective clothing, 14, *47*

Quicksilver, 56

Radiation, 11, 30–32, 42–44, 66; definition of, 42; and DNA, 43; patterns of, 42; sources of, 42
Radio waves, 42, 43
Radioactive fallout, 12
Radon, 38, 57–59; *map, 58*
Regulatory systems, 21–22
Resistance to disease, 18–21

Saccharin, 51
Safe Drinking Water Act of 1974, 37
Sanitation, 29–30
Selenium, 56
Shock, 24
Silicosis, 48, 66
Smoking, and fetus, 11
Sodium chloride, 51
Sodium nitrite, 51
Sound, as radiation, 42
Staphyloccus microorganism, 13
Sterility, 43

Stress, 13, 66
Sulfur dioxide, 38, 53
Sulfuric acid, 53
Surgeon General, U.S., 33–35
"Survival of the fittest," 18
Symptoms, of air pollution, 38; caused by allergens, *23*; of environmental disease, 9; of lead poisoning, 55

Technology, effect of, 61–62
Temperature, body, 21, 22
Toxin, 13, 66
Transmission electron micrograph (TEM), *51*
Typhoid, 29
Typhus, 29

Venereal (sexually transmitted) disease, 11
Vibrations of energy waves, 42–43
Vinyl chloride, 57
Viruses, and sickness, 13
Volatile organic compounds (VOCs), 59–60

Water, and transmission of disease, 29
WHO (World Health Organization), 29
Whooping cough, 21
World health problems, 29–30

X rays, *30*, 42